Open Country

# Open Country

## John Wain

HUTCHINSON

London   Melbourne   Auckland   Johannesburg

PR
6045
.A4
064
1987

This edition first published in 1987 by Hutchinson Ltd, an imprint of
Century Hutchinson Ltd, Brookmount House, 62–65 Chandos Place,
London, WC2N 4NW

Century Hutchinson Australia Pty Ltd,
PO Box 496, 16–22 Church Street, Hawthorn, Victoria 3122, Australia

Century Hutchinson New Zealand Limited,
PO Box 40-086, Glenfield, Auckland 10, New Zealand

Century Hutchinson South Africa Pty Ltd,
PO Box 337, Bergvlei, 2012 South Africa

Photoset by Rowland Phototypesetting Ltd,
Bury St Edmunds, Suffolk

Printed and bound in Great Britain by
Anchor Brendon Ltd, Tiptree, Essex

*British Library Cataloguing in Publication Data*
Wain, John
  Open Country.
  I. Title
  821'.914      PR6045.A249

  ISBN: 0-09-168261-4

# *Contents*

*Roger's*

# *Foreword*

I recognize two kinds of poem: the short, tightly organized kind that
hits a nail on the head, saying one thing (however multi-layered that
'one thing' may turn out to be) and saying it completely and memor-
ably; and the large-scale, grab-bag kind into which the poet can toss his
ideas, speculations, memories, prejudices, loves and hatreds as you
might toss the family's clothes into the washing machine, confident
that when they come out they will be at any rate fit to wear; and, if they
were any good to start with, not much shrunk or faded.

As regards form, the nail-on-the-head poem needs a strict con-
tainer, either one of the traditional forms that set up a specific
expectation and satisfy it, or an extemporized, *ad hoc* form which makes
the poem take a natural shape like that of a wild hawthorn bush
growing on a hillside: not regular or trimmed, but clearly organic and
with a reason why everything is where it is. (The trust-to-luck method
of most contemporary 'verse' is designed to hide, or evade, the fact that
this kind of improvised form is very, very difficult to write successfully.)
The grab-bag poem needs a metre informal enough to digest prose
information as easily as a goat digests thistles, so that there is no
laughable discrepancy between the formality of the verse and the
obstinate prosiness of the matter such as we get in a line like

Spade! with which Wilkinson hath tilled his ground.

Every poem I write is aimed at one or the other of these objectives. If it
is a sequence, there may be elements of both within the same work. But
it is fair to the reader to remark that the purest example of the grab-bag
poem I have written in recent years, a poem running to some eighteen
pages of typescript and entitled 'Something Nasty in the Greenhouse,'
turned out to tip the balance of this modest volume into too great a
length and has been held over for a future collection.

J.W.
Winter 1986/87

# *Acknowledgements*

These poems appeared in *The Antigonish Review*, Nova Scotia; *A Birthday Tribute to Charles Causley* (Enitharmon Press); *The Hudson Review*, New York; *Other Poetry*; *Poetry* Australia; *Voices*, Israel, and were published in separate form by The Pisces Press (*Poems for the Zodiac*); Bran's Head at the Hunting Raven Press (*Twofold*); The Celandine Press (*Midweek Period Return*), and *Through a Poet's Eye*, (Tate Gallery Publications), whose editors and publishers are thanked for permission to reprint.

# Twofold
## A Sequence of Fourteen Poems

1
Celebrating
a symbiosis:
taking note of a successful
graft or splice or inlay or dovetail
of the one nervous system with the other,
bringing unison, bringing two-moving-as-one:

and marvelling at

two spines, one vertical, one horizontal,
two brains, one carried low for finding out,
one carried aloft six feet above the stones:

thinking of the delicate
communication, the wordless talking,
the sharing of perception and impulse, the trusting,
the identification, the mutuality so endless
so difficult to pin down with a neat description
we might as well give up and call it love:

thinking of these things,
marvelling,
celebrating these things,
I will sing, I will sing.


2
They shape a moving geometry
a not-quite-fearful symmetry

his spine straight and tall
is the triangle's back wall

the taut leash the hypotenuse
her supple pads guiding his patient shoes

dictate the amalgam's progression
in calm Euclidean fashion

and as Euclid pondered
on forms that never wandered

beyond the reach of laws
hedged in like grazing cows

in necessity's green pastures
holding their logical postures

so thought with its true hold
plots the moves of Twofold

where impulses cluster
cool brain must be master

but the spirit's deep wells
nourish the brain-cells.


3
A duet of species finely performed, and also
an equally fine duet of genders, as I

imagine Twofold. Not, of course, inevitable:
some blind men must be led by male dogs, some blind

women by female dogs, some by male: still, most
guide-dogs are bitches, and in my mind's eye

for no better reason than being male myself
I see the upright partner as a man.

I see the female perception guiding the male
investigating, reacting, preparing the ground

for the steps he makes towards a planned destination.
I see the female in light, the male in darkness.

She is familiar with contour and contingency,
with events' texture, with corners' abruptness:

he builds in darkness a world of intentions:
landscapes blossom within that globe of shadow.

He wants to construct the world according to his needs:
she needs to want the world in order to construct.

His is the strength, the onward-driving passion,
hers is the guiding and sustaining element:

as some great whale migrating across the world
follows the path of a stream within the ocean.


4
I was little. Dam, warm coat,
smell of good. Smooth, naked dugs.
Tug, drink. Other me's, push
for a dug. Then roll. Paws.
Straw. Was there straw?

Standups took me to a strange place.
No straw. Boards. In the big air,
hardness: rough pads. Pavement,
they kept saying, Pavement.

Where did they go, the other me's?
Did dam stay there?
Is her coat still warm,
somewhere?
Does good smell the same?

11

I have a warm coat. But no
small me's. Standups gave me a sleep,
I woke up sick. After that,
dogs did not smell good:
dugs are somewhere else.
Pavement, pavement is my world.


5
I know smell-talk. A smell means *come,
sniff. Turn here. Stop. Sniff.*

Stand-ups told me No.
No smell.
Go forward. Dog-smell, man-smell,
sharp hunting cat-rabbit smell,
dustbin come-and-search smell,
earth-after-rain smell, saying *Dig,
scratch*: all No.

Go forward.
He has to go forward.
Standups do not know smell. It is not
their way of talking.
They use ears, eyes.
His ears. My eyes.
Go forward.


6
Safe: raised up
on a small cliff: steep quick sides
but short, easy. Yes, but big
in feeling. Down, trouble.
Danger. Fear. Could be the end
of light, warm. Could be crushed
broken bones, hurt. Up, good.

Up on the small cliff, feet-scuff.
Standups walking, slow, quick.
Trousers. Skirts with sway.
Skirts with no sway. Boots.
All move, a river of Standups,
to where the small cliff stops. *Now*:
Watch. Listen. Eyes up
for lights. Or a green Standup
walking in a round eye.

Mostly, no lights. Just look
for Rollers being still. They
are waiting to kill us.
Make them wait.
When Standups walk, walk.
To the next cliff. Slow
as you go up: his foot
feels for safe. Safe comes.


7
Till I was seven, I had sight.
Light and dark built alternate worlds
One, two, day, night, time's footfalls.
I know what a house looks like,
a tree, a hedge; table, chair,
man, woman. I know clouds.
I know what a dog looks like.
I know what my dog looks like.

She sees me. I do not see her.
She sees house, table, chair, tree,
hedge. She knows the closed eye of night,
the open of day.
                    But drably.
Her vision is monochrome, or nearly so.
I remember more sight than she sees.

I can recall the colour of butter,
eggs, bread, oranges. I can say *Red*
and watch red grow in the blackness,
flow, bloom, spread, fire to warm the world.
Yellow is a dancing daffodil trumpet.
Green is lying down in coolness. Blue, ah,
blue is my secret festival. When I
was five, I dipped a white stick in a tin
of blue paint, on our garage floor.
I took it out. It dripped and trailed: Blue,
it said, Blue, Joy in blue. Joy in blue.


8

She is programmed for work.
He is programmed for leisure, friends, talk, music
and work.

Her work is to walk Twofold.
His is the Law. In a house
with others, he sits in quiet
rooms. Trees swish outside. He has
the quietest office, at the back.

All the others have eyes. He, sound-bound
has the most need of quiet. His ears
need to be focussed, fenced from disturbance.

Tree-swish and (muffled beyond doors) keyboard-tap.

Sometimes, her sigh. Stretched out
beneath the desk, her warm flank close
to his still feet.
                    Work, work.

9
We journey to the big talk-kennel.
Hello-voices. Coffee-smell. Then the long
waiting, under the wood he rests his hands on.
Standups come in. He says, *Sit*.
He voices them. They voice him.
Often they use their sounds that are like ours,
their *that-hurts* whine, their *let-me-out* whine,
their alarm bark.

He voices on, always the same.
Easy, easy, quieting them.
They touch hands. They go.
More come.


10
They come to me to hear the law, to know
if the law will give them a little scope to live,
get someone off their back, even things out.

They have eyes, usually two per person, that drink
in the blessing of colour, the joy of light,
but colour and light are blurred by a crust of sorrow.

Their eyes serve as the gathering-point of tears
and when they look, it is with greed and fear
at what another has.
                      For my own part,

I do not seem to have much greed and fear.
My sorrow is channelled into one deep well.
I have not many grudges to avenge.

At my approach, people become more gentle.
They put away the clubs and the long knives
they use on one another: as if they thought

15

to be blinded is already club and knife,
enough to bear.

                       And so they sit and weep,
and stutter out the tale of loss and outrage
that brings them to my door. And I sit here,
calm, taking notes with subtle finger-tips,

Who knows injustice better than I? Knows better
simply what happens is the force that rules?
Yet I explain the law, the law, the law.


11
August. A velvet night.
They tell me the moon is full.
I lie awake, throw back the covers, feel
on my skin the cleanness of the air.
That means the world outside
is flooded with the moon's calm light.

I feel the clarity:
I listen to the light. A bell-tower
chimes over there, beyond the orchard.

Waves of bell-sound come to me over sleeping
apple-boughs. I hear her twitch an ear:
it almost wakes her, almost communicates
some message: but what could it be?

Does she know what a bell is?
Does she know what apples are?
Not as I know them: yet they say
wild dogs, and even some that live in kennels,
howl when the moon is full.

## 12

Evening. It is feeding-time for both.
Others will set food before him, but first
he feeds her.

The tin, in its expected place.
Round, smooth, heavy. One knowing hand,
the left, holds it table-steady: the right
drives in the harsh diminutive
sword-point of the tin-opener. Press, turn:
press, turn: a jagged circle falls
clean out. Repeat other end. Now push
a cylinder of meat and sliding fat
into her waiting dish.

Now crush in biscuits, scraps. A swill of milk.
He feels her waiting, hears her looking up.

So: place the dish. Then soap and towel.
Clean hands. Now it is his turn to be fed.

But as she licks and swallows, he is aware
she nourishes for him. Nerve-impulses,
blood-density, soft marrow and hard bone,
satellite brain. Her pads are his fore-toes.
Her rough pelt sprouts from his scalp. Her eyes
are his two eyes, on snail-stalks.

The tin of meat he neatly circles out
feeds him. He murmurs grace.

13

They call the day over, lie down in attitudes
of relinquishment. Sleep folds in both spheres.

Singly, they lie, each exploring the individual
labyrinth of unconsciousness, wired to contrasting
diagrams. She patrols a thicket of residual
day-actions, brittle as firewood. His more lasting

sleep-catacombs, fanged with memory's stalactites,
invite sober pacing, abound in rounded opaque
metaphor. Nothing connects their two nights
except the slumber that rounds them like a coiled snake,

unhitching their duality, refreshing them with a respite
of singleness. When light wakes them, all the more
willingly they build themselves back into Twofold:
connect, gear in, dance to their unheard music.


14

As grateful as the hand that warms the glove
their pliancy of trust. Has it a name?
We might as well give up and call it love.

This mutuality I'm thinking of
as double as two windows in one frame
is grateful as the hand that warms the glove.

Such woven trust of two, what does it prove?
Is it a dance, a combat or a game?
We might as well give up and call it love.

What eye can count the wing-beats of a dove?
Their rapid impulse-sharing is the same,
as grateful as the hand that warms the glove.

Gentle as leaves that whisper in a grove,
sudden as sparks that whirl above a flame:
we might as well give up and call it love.

Though strict neurology may disapprove,
I had to use the only words that came:
as grateful as the hand that warms the glove.
We might as well give up and call it love.

# Poems for the Zodiac

Among the treasures of the Bodleian Library is a wonderful fifteenth-Century French Book of Hours. I would not have had the enterprise to discover it for myself, but fortunately the Library issued a set of twelve postcards for sale at the stall in the main entrance; these show the sign of the zodiac on one side, and on the other the appropriate human tasks for that season of the year – carrying water, mowing, threshing and so on.

The poems were first published as twelve separate *feuilletons*, for which Brenda Stones of Pisces Press created illustrations from the original illuminations, to show the dual content of each poem. They have (in case anyone should approach them with that kind of expectation) nothing to do with astrology, either in its classic or debased form.

# Aquarius – Janus feasting

The richly clothed man looks both ways: his dual
palate tastes wine and meat, his brain defines
north – south, east – west, his delicate renewal.

The almost naked man, whose toil combines
humility with mastery, seems content:
he tilts his generous urn while Janus dines.

Water, the indivisible element,
moves without strain wherever it is beckoned.
This tells us what the world's creation meant:

the seas were the first feast, the rocks the second.
Janus is right to smile in two directions,
for water made his sunny fields grow fecund:

rain-cloud and harvest are the two perfections.

# Aries – Trimming vines

Vines, when pollarded,
are not unlike toy willows. The old wood
roots, and swells to a dark gnarled fist: the new,
thin, supple and ochre, climbs devotedly
up iron stakes.
        The ram, too, is a toy,
a woolly toy that children take to bed.
His amber eyes are like glass marbles, his coat
a laughable mop for rain-soak and sun-steam.

God's toys, though. Man's work. Implicit in the vine
the steady pruning-knife and careful eye.
Behind the ram's bounding, the sleepless shepherd,
the watchful crouch of the black-and-white dog.

And all this, in the eye of the wild spring sun!

# Pisces – Burning firewood

Two fish, connected by a loving cord.
They love each other, and they praise the Lord

who shaped them clean and cold and undramatic,
not mammal, not amphibious, but aquatic.

Here is a fish wish: may your lovely scales
shine calm as pearls where $H_2O$ prevails:

in the cold month that chains men by the grate
we'll hear the call of love, and procreate:

embrace by rubbing torso against torso,
as sensual as phalluses, but more so:

till I release my spawn and you your eggs.
Why need we envy lovers who have legs?

In warm spring water we will hatch our fry:
if twenty live, let twenty million die.

And when the land in summer sunshine cooks,
may every angler swallow his own hooks!

# Taurus – Carrying a green branch

The young bull stands in the new grass. His shoulders
are hard with the same strength as the river, the trees
and the mountain. His breath blows sweet.
The globes of his seed hang behind his belly:
the young heifers will bring him their gentleness,
large-eyed and delicate-hoofed

                         O be glad of him,
celebrate his joyfulness in the lust of the young year:
display your green branch, let it wave to and fro,
as his dewlap waves when his great head swings!

# Gemini – Hawking

Twins: wearing that subtle yoke
since their first dawn broke.

Man and bird: one fierce will
to recognize and kill.

Brothers in gentle play
have joy in their brief May.

The hawk must ride hooded,
his wild nature secluded.

The brothers wrestle and fall,
their laughter sweetens all.

Man and hawk are twinned:
they wheel in the one wind.

The brothers pause for breath:
the loosed hawk deals death.

# Cancer – Mowing

The crab eats the dead. He wears armour.
He does not voyage far. Leisurely, plated,
he patrols the one beach.

Pisces, beware Cancer. Avoid his claw.
He moves sidelong.

The young grasses wave in the sunlight.
Their slender blades tremble: with joy, we think,
with new-summer joy, like us. But the man
with the scythe says *No*,
*it is fear. The grass is rooted,*
*it can dance but it cannot escape.*

He can afford to move slowly.
He also patrols the one field, he also
moves sidelong.

# Leo – Reaping

The great cat's mane is a field of wind-stirred wheat:
he is the lion, who knows death but not defeat.

The man with the sickle bends to work with a smile
happy that hunger and death are held off awhile

for the Maker has blessed the ground with resurgence of crops.
The two hands of His power were the sunlight and the raindrops,

and the lion, imagined by this painter who had never seen one,
smiles too, as if glad that a gold season has flamed from a green one;

and the French painter has the lion walking in a green field,
scratching it with one clawed foot for the cool scent it will yield:

and he has linked the beast's crown with the crown of the earth:
for art exists to remind us in feast and in dearth

that man is in nature and obeys the natural law
though his instructed hand is stronger than the lion's paw

and that beast and man exist by permission of sun and rain:
though man's fate is always to learn this and forget it again.

27

# Virgo – Threshing

The wheat is ripe. Now thresh it. Make it pure.
No stalk, no leaves, no chaff: only the gold
grains plumped-out and pristine, fit for good bread.

That girl approaching with her sober tread
is called Virginity. Her touch is cold.
She lies alone. Her body must endure

hunger and frost. Yet love that knows no cure
for craving lust has also tears to shed.
She shines above. We, in that torrent rolled,

look up. Her calm is lovely to behold.
And yet her agony is not less sure.
Even as the wheat is flailed, her heart has bled.

# Libra – Treading grapes

The crushed grape breaks its skin:
wine-making can begin.

She holds the scales up high:
*do, and be done by.*

Wine is no accident.
It comes by a true descent:

the scales, the measuring,
the eye for a fine thing.

Soil, weather, time: this fruit
wears knowledge at its root:

measure that rules all things,
as in a bird's spread wings,

joining a poor man's task
to the justice we all ask.

The patient feet are treading.
The matched scales are a wedding.

# Scorpio – Sowing

The green shoot learns to climb.
Cold poison waits its time.

Flesh fears the scorpion
bone moves back from his dry touch
spirit shuns all such.

Flesh-hunger applauds the sower
bone's patience shares his toil
hope is spirit's lamp-oil.

Flesh, bone and spirit know
death and life both must grow,
grain swell, poison flow.

The seed is a secret thing.
So is the sting.

# Sagittarius – Feeding pigs

The oak is the noblest tree. It lives
calm-rooted through men's troubled centuries.
An acorn is magic. We call a man a conjurer
who can pull a rabbit out of a top hat:
why, Nature pulls an oak tree out of an acorn!

These pellets of time and strength, these
crunchy woody morsels of miracle, to be
the favourite food of cheerfully rooting pigs!
Of grunting, belly-selfish, prosaic mammals!

And the man with the pole knocks them down in clusters
as if he thought it all very ordinary:
as if oak-sap and bacon-fat were somehow the same.

As indeed they are, for Nature is a priestess.
Her simplest routines are aflame with mystery.

So how can the half-man, half-horse archer surprise us?
To believe an acorn is to believe anything.

# Capricorn – Slaughtering

The innocent calf succumbs to the butcher's knife.
This death (the man thinks) I inflict in the name of life.

For we become long-lived through infanticide.
It is the mild flesh of the young and untried

(leaves that have never known the pinch of frost,
beasts with their size and strength in a future now lost)

that we swallow in our unresting hunt for survival.
Meanwhile the billy-goat, egotist without rival,

displays his proud horns amid (in December!) green leaves:
he is the professional survivor who never grieves.

Only kids are eaten, he knows. Once past that stage
the goat trots on to a satisfied old age:

with flesh too tough and rank for the cooking-pot
he lives on where summer is fresh and goat-blood hot.

He leads the sheep-flock, his wife gives nourishing milk.
He has no objection to usefulness of that ilk,

but to hold still while someone cuts your throat
is simply not consistent with being a goat.

# Mid-Week Period Return
## Home Thoughts of a Native

This poem was commissioned by Mr Roger Pringle, whose Celandine Press in Stratford-upon-Avon was bringing out a volume of verse tributes to John Betjeman. I had published a severe review of *Summoned by Bells* about twenty years earlier and had ever since seen myself mentioned among Betjeman's 'attackers,' 'decriers,' etc., whereas in fact I had come through the years to have a much higher opinion of his poetry; so I threw myself into the writing of a poem for him, in topographical vein, with such enthusiasm that the result, as Mr Pringle pointed out when he received it, was amusingly too long. If he had printed it there would have been no room in the book for anything else. He solved the problem by printing a short extract in the commissioned volume and bringing out the complete text, with drawings by Arthur Keene, in 1982.


I took the railway from Oxford to Stoke-on-Trent
and JB was with me every mile I went.

These are the two towns that mean most to me
where I have lived longest and feel most free

from the cramps and constrictions of this our dour epoch
since each in its own way has managed to stop the clock

enough to celebrate in sharply contrasting scenes
some rearguard victory of the men over the machines:

and I looked out of the window as the train clattered along
and felt JB's presence always persistent and strong

for he loves England and holds her in his heart
though like me he has had to watch her body torn apart

and her spirit travestied and misunderstood
in our age of lasting evil and evanescent good.

In fact I think of Betjeman very often:
his deftly-drawn images have refused to fade or soften

and some of them have been with us for fifty years.
There is an instinctive truth in the course he steers.

I have found things in his work to praise and blame:
most literate people could probably say the same.

But he speaks to me always of England, her follies and bounties.
He is a presence in London, in the Home Counties,

in Pembrokeshire or Lincoln or on the Berkshire downs,
but most of all in Oxford, ravaged queen of towns,

where he went to school and felt young life unfolding,
not yet foreseeing the nightmares of William Golding.

He knows his Oxford, his young eyes were among the last
to see her stately with the beauty that changed to past

on the day Morris opened his factory in Cowley:
William Morris! Irony of his being so named, who foully

shattered the centuries-old balance of Tillage and Thought
by throwing across it a new city that could never be taught

the secrets of either, the incurable infection
of a clumsy transplant resulting in tissue rejection.

I have never hated Morris, nor felt unforgiving
about a man who simply wanted a living

for himself and others, to keep the job-wires humming:
still, anyone with normal vision could have seen it coming,

and it would not have hurt Morris to have been persuaded
to build up his industry where it could have been aided

by an existing work-force and industrial tradition,
instead of committing moral and aesthetic sedition,

however unconsciously, by letting his monster loose
to wring the neck of Oxford like a Christmas goose

waddling on Port Meadow all the years I remember
then suddenly disappearing about mid-December

to hang in the poulterers' shops as Oxford hangs now.
These thoughts weigh on me as the train pulls past the Plough

Inn at Wolvercote where I drink, and past my own
house, a scribbled-over-with-green box of stone,

and as the train gathers speed and leaves Oxford behind
they hang like chill stalactites from the roof of my mind.


1
On my journey I paid little attention to churches
and none to suburbs with paving and silver birches

but I always had a loving eye for canals and rivers
which are arteries and boundaries and importance-givers.

In the Cherwell Valley there are two water-courses
each with its own way of obeying nature's forces.

The canal lies in a series of rational grand curves
following the land's contours. With delighted dashes and swerves

the river offers a sweet wilful parody of that logic,
making its rationality seem bland and pedagogic,

now coming so close as to share the same fringe of reeds,
now withdrawing in pursuit of its own secret needs.

Rejoice in it, rejoice while it is still to be seen,
while the soft grey sky brings out the richness of the green,

for the men who want to make all England a speedway for heavy
 trucks
are planning to murder the grass and the willows, the reeds and the
 swimming ducks,

and when the bulldozers come the Cherwell Valley will go:
and the fouled river struggling on somewhere below

and the choked canal canopied in noise and fumes
will have died for our England that consumes, consumes, consumes.


*The train rattles and sways, then the train slows,*
*to halt at another place this poet knows.*

Leamington. The metal python-loops of the bridge
slide by. Below, a glimpse of the street, and shops.
There used to be a bookshop there, where I once

bought a set of Dickens (Chapman and Hall) and a book
that had belonged to Philip Larkin (*Characters*
*of the Seventeenth Century*, ed. Nichol Smith, Oxford, 1920; why

did he sell it?). The young JB used to take
the train here from Oxford for the afternoon,
walk about and look at the buildings: wrote

one of his best poems about it, 'Death
in Leamington'. With a more urgent tremor I recall
this is where the train from Stratford starts and ends.

It loiters from station to station, names like Bearley
and Wilmcote, fields and lanes and hillsides
I have seen many times, but always in summer,

so that to me it is the English summer train,
cottage gardens with loaded fruit-trees, roadside grass
standing tall and feathery, with dandelions and rust-red

sorrel heads. And then Stratford!, wide open
of course to the tourist industries of the world, but still
with the flavour of a market town, and really an unusual

number of Tudor buildings, not all on show
with clicking turnstiles. Some people, nose in air, have
'no patience with Stratford'. I have no patience with

people who have no patience with Stratford, partly
because it was the magic place of my youth,
where with young friends I wandered on summer evenings

or in dew-fresh mornings before the coaches came,
and partly because in that big red-brick barn
they act out his stories, his singing parables.

Through the stretched-out years, on pin-pointed evenings,
hat and coat folded under the seat, souvenir programme
in hand, I have sat with switched-on eyes and ears:

taking in the nightingale grief of Juliet,
the tall dignity of Othello's pain,
or Shylock with his rigid Old Testament soul

seeing revenge and law and a daughter's obedience
in the stark primary colours of the Middle East:
and Autolycus has sung and Falstaff laughed and groaned.

*The train rattles and sways, then the train slows,*
*to halt at another place this poet knows.*

Nobody praises Birmingham. At least
if praise exists, I haven't come across it.
And yet the place rouses in me no real
hostility, no scorn or deep revulsion:
nothing to prompt me to a satire like
'Come, friendly bombs, and fall on Slough' (how well
I can recall the shiver of fierce joy
which seized me when I came across that line
while still at school, the comradeship of knowing
that someone else hated the things I hated).

No, I could never write a 'Slough' about
flaccid old Brum, nor, I suspect, could he.
A lot of honest work has gone on there,
mostly in metal, and there have been artists:
Burne-Jones and William Morris (the real one),
and John Henry Newman, and behind them
the young Sam Johnson finding himself a wife.

And in our time, the University:
A. M. D. Hughes discoursing on Literature
(a man of the rarest cultivation of mind)
and the young Helen Gardner in his department,
and teaching classics, the young Louis MacNeice
(patient of 'Homer in a Dudley accent'), and Auden
growing up just outside, at Solihull.
The light has never gone completely out.
No, Birmingham is not quite Slough or Uxbridge.

*Clearer than Scafell Pike, my heart has stamped on*
*The view from Birmingham to Wolverhampton.*

So wrote the Auden of the youthful English mind
before he left our way of thinking behind

and moved to where the people were strangers and the open spaces
really were open, where the dour vigilant faces

of his own tribe were no longer there to accuse him
though in their devoted hunger to exploit and use him

his new hosts proved even more expert at removing his scalp
till he had to hide away on top of an Austrian alp

where people would leave him alone to get his breath,
and finally came back to Oxford to wait for death.

Well, it is over now, and as the train pulls past
blank windows and canal sluices I can reconcile at last

the minor Atlantic Goethe whose hobby was theology
and the schoolboy so bright-eyed about mining and geology.

Now the menhirs of industrial pre-history slide by,
the eighteenth century crumbles under a Diesel-thick sky:

This part of Birmingham is called Soho, a better spectacle
even in its ruin than London's brim-full receptacle

of all the detritus of flaked skin, toenails and vomit
left when millions share a cold sexual dream and from it

never quite manage to wake. The acres of wrecked cars
rusting in the Midland rain are at least better than the bars

full of pimps and transvestites and lonely ostriches
with heads in the muddy sand between neon-lit ditches.

About mid-point one seems to sense a thinning
of the rails and sheds and tips, almost the beginning

of a trampled mud-patch of country, here a strip of grazing
for a horse, there a chicken run, but so far from phasing

down, the industrial tangle resumes at once: Wolverhampton
is part of the tarnished breastplate Birmingham has clamped on.


*The train rattles and sways, then the train slows,*
*and now we have left the England this poet knows,*

because from Wolverhampton we move through Stafford to Stoke
where JB's Victorian connoisseurship seems a joke

in another language, and his Anglican piety
a conjuring trick in the old twice-nightly variety.

Yet his or not, it is England, and he must
be aware what good things lie beneath clay-slip and coal-dust.

> My city was built for a wedding,
> nave, aisle and altar:
> the bride and the bridegroom are treading
> a dance without falter.
>
> He shines black, she pale as a moon:
> she is kneaded, he broken.
> But their strength is united, and soon
> the blessing is spoken.
>
> The coal fires the clay, the clay
> shines back to the coal:
> and the man in his brief passing day
> adds his touch to the whole.

This marriage is important and also complex and strange:
between them the parties cover almost the whole range

of forms of being. He began as vegetation,
trunks, bark, leaves, roots: untold aeons of gestation

and millions of tons of rock-pressure were needed
to evolve his glossed brittleness and stored warmth. She proceeded

by an even more surprising route: basically stone
milled by incalculable time to a paste, but also bone,

the skulls, limbs and rib-cages of vegetarian beasts,
powdered and mixed in till translucency increased

and with it tensile strength, the resistance to impact.
So the groan-haunted slaughterhouse plays its part, and in fact

both coal-mine and pot-bank are slaughterhouses too:
miners are trapped and entombed, and of potters a few

have always let in death through their mouths and noses:
my father's father died of potter's silicosis.

And now I get out and stand beside the train
happy to see that steeple-crowned hill again,

the tall church in whose shadow I learnt to read
the miraculous black marks that answered my deepest need.

In the moving crowd I stand, a silent, grateful man,
since this place, for me, is where it all began.

Here, coal and clay come together to breed a city
where life is strong and resilient though never pretty,

and this city is where the story began for me,
and still goes on. This poem is for JB.

# George Orwell, in Barcelona, Imagines Jura

Cold air from the mountains.
This thin tunic was someone else's. I should
have got kitted out properly: a British Warm
(going cheap any time since I was fifteen,
good Cotswold wool, none of this Southern trash,
discipline stitched into every seam:
something left to us by those straight-backed men
who disappeared into the mud): I might have felt
as if I were on active service then,
not playing soldiers with this bunch of clowns
half comic, half pathetic. Brave though, brave.
Shall I be brave like them, when the clear air
sings loud with bullets? when the cold peaks look down
on bodies sprawled as I remember them
in the *Illustrated London News* when I was twelve,
belly down on the carpet before the fire,
chin on my elbows, turning the shiny pages,
aghast at finding what grown men had to do.

A time of beginnings. Hope blowing in the air,
Hope for what? To be done, I suppose, with greed:
greed that can afford to buy death and wounds:
greed rich enough to collect the toys of power –
steel gratings, sound-proof cells, and men
who feel secure in uniform.

Sometimes, in the night, I feel we might as well
try to break down the mountains that stand round
or empty out the sea.
                              Yet, after all,
there was a time before the mountains were:
and even the sea is just a bowl of salt.

We have to press on. They attack. We attack. There is
no stopping. It is a set of iron wheels
that cannot stop till something is chewed up.
Who will be chewed to nothing? We or they?

No one knows yet. It will be decided.
That is what we are here for, to decide it.


These chopped-straw cigarettes make me cough. But the air,
in its coldness, floods my chest like hope.
The incitement of melting snow: a time
of beginnings. What did the blind man write?
'Or breath of vernall air from snowie Alpe.'
The scattered detritus of that education
they worked so long to give me.

One day, one day, I will go back to it.

One day, if our side wins. One day, if this
iron time ever passes, when the puppets
can put on the mobile faces of men and women
and the soft, rounded, growing limbs of children:
when greed and war are beaten to a standstill
or pursued with demons to some other planet
to hatch their empires there: one day, I shall
be at peace under a roof of sloping stones,
with fowl pecking outside, and the sea's voice:
a different sea from the hard dark line out there
that slices at the sky with its cutting edge:
a sea with tides, and rock-basins, and seals.
And then I shall mix myself a fuller palette
beyond these blacks and whites and greys, if that
day comes.

                    Yes, then I shall go back.
to a life more simple than this of war, and more complex.
All my books so far have been calls to action.
In that stone house with a stack of turf outside
I shall build some shelves, and on the highest one,
almost out of reach even for me,

I shall store my call-to-action books. Not so
as to disown them, just to say *Their war
is over. Stand at ease, good soldiers
whose long day's fighting has earned a quiet shelf.*

The firelight will play on their faded jackets,
and I shall turn to a stack of new white sheets.
No more clarion-calls. The work I shall be about
will have the calm of a boulder on the shore,
the colour and fragrance of the hillside gorse,
and its perceptions will be sharp as peat-smoke.
These fine shades incite to action, of a kind.

Or to the slow maturing of attitudes:
the subsoil, the peat, from which action will form itself:
the long slow maturation, the root-fibres.

But nothing realised in one generation.

But the colours of intimidation are primary.
Threatened people must act before nightfall.
What drove me always to herd with the threatened?
Whatever that force was, I welcome it.
I welcome kinship with the gaunt and ragged.
I eat the proffered crust. They can have
my carcase if it will be of any use.

But the nuances? The shifting colours?
We all have them, even these people have them,
in the hours when they rest and listen to the grasshoppers:
If those hours came to them more often
I could rest too, I could hear the grasshoppers.
And then the characters I draw in outline
could be filled in. Spirit, breath, and being.

I know what they say about me. I make puppets,
and art is about people.

But puppets act,
they jerk their limbs and throw themselves about,
dance, perform tasks, then knock each other flat.
They act when someone pulls their strings. Who pulls?
Over there, among the mountain peaks,
the Fascists pull. Down here, we pull: the ones
who keep alive some dream of kindliness.
Oh, I could give my life to chiaroscuro,
and the rainbow-trout colours of sensibility
and I could do it with a clear conscience
because there is a fullness of truth in it.
Wholeness of life is complex: when I tell
my puppet stories I am simplifying.
But life itself, in our time, simplifies.
Hunger, imprisonment, beatings are simplicities.
The thugs have robbed the people. And one of the things
they have robbed them of is their complexity.


Those English writers contemplating choices!
Virginia wondering who will go to the lighthouse
and for what finely balanced reasons . . . I respect her,
as I respect a painter who gives years
to catching the swirl of a stream beneath a bridge,
or the slant of light on a London chimney-pot.

I am with the people who are robbed,
forced to live the simplicities of animals.
One day, both they and I will shed that starkness,
if our side wins. I shall have a stone house,
whitewashed, and coloured fowl pecking outside.
There will be no disdainful Pyrenees,
just stony, rounded hills, the home of curlews.
The sea will talk to itself, and I shall listen.
The fowl will cluck, and drawl. I shall sit watching
the sky change colour as the clouds move over.

45

# George Orwell, in Jura, Imagines Barcelona

It seems so long since I saw a lizard.
These rocks have never been hot:
not since the first volcano.

Strange that Eileen should have died first.
There are no simplicities among these mists.
This is Fingal's country.

Sitting at tables in the Ramblas:
small, bitter cups of black coffee.
Eileen would remember that.

Small, bitter cups also of betrayal.
Hot sunlight defining each tile
on the roof of the telephone exchange.

The Ramblas between us and the Guardia Civil.
Roof-top to roof-top.
We agreed not to fire.

Behind them was the coiled spring of Hitler.
Four years later London was burning.
Bricks too hot for a lizard.

Paving-stones too hot for a scorpion:
and I saw the dead people again,
as in the *Illustrated London News*.

Strange that Eileen should have died first.
The Fascists were trying to get me.
They got her.

She died in their fascist war.
Bombs, fatigue, not enough to eat:
she grew white and weary.

Strange that Eileen should have died first.
She loved me in the days of simplicities.
She sent cigars to the Lenin barracks.

In that hard vertical light
simplicities grew: ideals, a shared smoke,
a bullet through the neck.

Now, here, the light is evanescent
as even Virginia could have wished,
(and she is dead too).

This is Fingal's country.
In these mists that coil and thin
I could believe in sea-serpents.

Last nightfall, looking from the headland
to where the spray mates with the mist
in the shimmer of the sunset colours,

a dark hump seemed about to surface.
Was it only a rock below the tide?
I expected a talking whale.

There are no seals in the Mediterranean;
lizards lie on the hot rocks.
Legends of mermaids are Atlantic.

The big grey father seals
look dog-like in the water,
but turn their heads and stare like men.

I think of the surf-haunting dugong,
a ton of clumsy mammal
wallowing in collapsing waves.

In Barcelona, I was a dugong.
I wallowed along the Ramblas
while the quick lizards peered out.

I was a talking whale
haloed in my own mist and spray.
Now I, too, am dying.

# Poem from an Inscription

In the pleasant Norman town of Bayeux, in the lee of the great Cathedral that was for centuries the home of the Tapestry (it is now in a special exhibition centre), stands the Hôtel de Ville. On its wall is a stone inscription, beautifully and movingly carved, containing the names of those hereabout who were war-time victims of the Gestapo. The foot of the inscription is occupied by a bas-relief of an emaciated corpse; its centre by a poem. I don't know who wrote the poem, though the City Fathers of Bayeux must know since the monument can hardly have been up more than forty years. I copied it into my notebook, but that was not enough to make its tragic beauty lie tamely in my mind; it went on fermenting until in desperation I tried to put the poem into my own language.

> *Qu'importe comment s'appelle*
> *Cette clarté sur leur pas*
> *Que l'un fut de la chapelle*
> *Et l'autre s'y dérobât*
> *Celui qui croyait au ciel*
> *Celui qui n'y croyait pas*
> *Tous les deux étaient fidèles*
> *Des lèvres, du coeur, des bras*
> *Et tous les deux disaient qu'elle*
> *Vive et qui vivra verra*
> *Celui qui croyait au ciel*
> *Celui qui n'y croyait pas*
> *Quand les blés sont sous la grêle*
> *Fou qui fait le délicat*
> *Fou qui songe à ses querelles*
> *Au coeur du commun combat*
> *Celui qui croyait au ciel*
> *Celui qui n'y croyait pas.*

What matter the name we give
to the all-revealing light
in which henceforth they live
or that one drew faith from the sight
of the steepled church on high
and the other walked heedless by?

They held to their faith, each one
in the way that came unsought
acknowledged that truth will live on
and wisdom at last be taught
though one saw God's face on high
and the other the empty sky.

When the storms thrash down the crop
who thinks of his petty spites?
Who acts the delicate fop
when beside his brothers he fights?
Not he who saw empty sky
nor he who saw God on high.

# Victor Neep 1921–1979

1
I am not tempted to an elegy of sorrow:
I shall see Victor when I wake tomorrow

as I saw him when I woke this morning:
his rich deep laughter will erupt without warning

from some unsupervised corner of my mind
at each new casual proof that the world was designed

by a Creator who evidently felt the need
to sow comicality like a rank unkillable weed

on every patch of experience, Victor's and mine
and yours. Of course the boundary-line

between laughter and tears is at its clearest very sketchy:
I do not know whether the Creator was being merely tetchy

or opening some deep vein of *recherché* black humour
by killing a man as creative as Victor with a brain tumour.

But before I make up my mind about that I must wait
and see how it feels when I encounter my own fate:

No one has any direct experience of being dead,
and perhaps the cliché is true, they have just moved ahead:

death claims people, but not totally, they are always there
ready to move towards the living through shadowy air,

and we are all on the way to that same destination:
but his paintings will give strength to a new generation.

2
A neep is a turnip. So what?
Pasternak is a parsnip. Some of the most creative
English people have had names like Bacon,
Lamb, Hogg: Keats was in love
with a girl called Brawne, and even Hazlitt
is a cheap kind of cooked meat.
A neep at least is a vegetable,
at home in the earth, and
it grows substantial, plump, authoritative,
by calm non-violent accretion,
peaceably ingesting the earth's moisture,
soil, rainfall, photosynthesis: all these
are gentle compared with an animal's fated
compulsion to eat other animals, or at best
to mangle leaves and roots. The vegetables
are the only philosophers, needing no religion
(why should they have a saviour? A Messiah?).
A turnip is a Buddha, rounded, serene,
complete within itself.
                              And then the colour!
luminously drab, excitingly commonplace, festively
respectable, that near-brown off-purple mat
finish. Yes, vegetables are saints,
and turnips with their heroic modesty
have a special place in that calendar: they merit
praise like Hopkin's sonnet on St Alphonsus
Rodriguez, if I could write like that.

Looked at another way,
and without in the least detracting from its sainthood,
a turnip is the product of engineering:
genetic engineering among vegetables.
It saved English agriculture in the eighteenth century,
it allowed people to drink milk in the winter
and withstand the climate better; it is the reason

why we have a tradition of eating beef
instead of veal like the Continentals;
Victorians believed this had given us the strength
to win the Battle of Waterloo,
thus becoming top dogs for a hundred years.
I wouldn't go that far,
and yet I think a neep is an honourable name:
and whatever associations it had before,
it is an illustrious name now, and in the future,
because it is Victor's name.


3
Where a man comes from and where he goes to
must be bound up with the inner frame of his being,
his flesh, his sorrows, his needs, the love-debt he owes to

a specific soil, clouds, rain falling on the trees,
and perhaps also to specific pavements and shops,
the roofs and windows and walls where we swarm like bees.

This artist was born in the flat industrial east
midlands, and ended amid the springing light
of the western sea and the mountains: yet of his life's feast

a main course always, a nutriment to his mind,
was the engineer's appreciation of metal and movement:
he never made the mistake of leaving behind

the factory with its low sheds and precision tools.
He saw nature in contrivance and contrivance in nature,
in steady waterfalls and rotating smoothed-out pools.

If he had a special tenderness for broken machines
slowly going back to the earth on hillside tips,
that was because a factory is the means

of bringing machines to birth: a compassionate eye
on birth, on the struggling entrance of something new,
understands that the something will one day have to die,

knows beginning and ending with that same compassion.
From the humming factory the machines journeyed to the still
    mountain,
becoming natural objects in their own fashion:

rained on and whistled through by the wind, forgotten,
having served their day: serving again as his symbols,
for he had been where contrivances are begotten,

amid intellectual and physical heat, amid stress
and exultation: his relish for the work of man's
quick inventive hand did not leave him with any less

love of stone, water and lichen, or make him less in tune
with the unwavering mysteries: how often, through the years,
did he paint that dark sky and mist-encircled moon?


4
I seem, looking back, to have done a lot of writing
about artists: the penalty, no doubt,
of living my life in the middle and later stretches
of the twentieth century,

when the last waves of religious faith are sinking
into the sands of materialism, and politics
has dwindled to a mere jockeying for advantage:
when ordinary men

have abandoned belief and pride in ordinary work,
when scientific research is tied to money and weapons
and the universities ruled by Whitehall accountants:
and only the artist

seems to have vision and freshness. Is this because
in a time of divided impulse, the artist can find
a source of vitality in the division itself,
a creative tension

between forces which, straining in opposite ways, can
build in the centre a space that the mind can inhabit,
if it is that kind of mind, inquisitive, supple,
not asking for comfort?

Victor was made up of opposites: his nightmares forced him
often to keep the light on all night, and his personal
vision of the abyss never quite left his thoughts, but always
he joked and was cheerful:

he fed on parties and binges, was always the last
to leave a good thrash, so that one's mental picture
shows him with a glass in his hand, but I never remember
seeing him drunk:

he needed the loneliness of the mountain nightfall,
the cry of a single sea-bird along the unpeopled
shore, and he needed the smoke-filled noisy room
with music and laughter,

needed them not in predictable alternation
like a pendulum, but held in his own amalgam:
carrying with him a frisson of either one
into the other.

Dear Victor, the world will go on in its lolloping fashion,
phonies and liars will prosper, thugs will have power,
but your voice will echo among the objects you painted.
See you tomorrow.

# Sea-Lanes
## Birthday Poem for Charles Causley

All those small harbours, fretted from the rock
of our dour coastline by the slurping sea,
we know them in brown-shadowed photographs
as they were then:

when did they change so totally? Strange, now,
that windows, walls and roofs we are looking at
are still there just as the antique lens held them:
the harbour office,

the tiered cottages, the steeple on the hill,
these still remain: but what of the human tide,
heavy with pods and salt, that washed about them?
Hardly a sailor

comes to these places now. The tides are there,
the jetty, clock, and lighthouse, but the ships
have gone to the breaker's yard. Ranged, confident,
in the sepia weather

we can still study that tangle of masts and spars,
and as the decades pass, the churning steamers,
smoke-stacks trained on the sky. Round them, oared craft
jostle like minnows:

and if by staring at it with sufficient
intensity, we could will ourselves back into
one of those scenes aglow with Victoria's sunset,
we'd find the fish-scaled

streets that climb from water-line to sky
echoing with sailors' voices, deep-sea talk:
the blue reek of their twist clouding pub windows,
and off the Horn

or in the fog and icebergs of St John's
or swaying clutched in the Sargasso weed,
old men with fine-meshed wrinkles edging their eyes
from scanning distances

would live it all again. For the last time,
as it turned out: their tribe became extinct
in less than half a lifetime. Why? The usual
reason: Technology,

dragging its heavy chain of money, crawled
resistless and unresting over their charts,
their memoried skill, their clustered masts, their talk.
The banker followed

where the inventor led, as he always does:
small ships are uneconomic: only the monsters,
carrying grotesque amounts, using a few
deep-water ports,

computerized neo-Swiftian floating islands,
ugly, forbidding, remote, outward expressions
of greed and the anxiety that nurtures greed,
stolidly pounding

across the oceans of the world, till something
goes wrong and they break in half (a heavy sea
finding the weakness in that stretched-out spine)
and sailors drown,

and the black oil pours out to sink the birds
and suffocate the seals, and the insurers
pay up, and another cliff-tall hull is launched.
The grove of masts

that grew in the green water of the harbours
went down under the axe of Money/Progress:
the sailors, beached, were dwindled into folk-lore,
like Captain Cat,

then vanished. (The folk-lore stage might have been spared.)
Now if Money and Progress were all that mattered,
as city board-rooms think it is, that would
have been the end.

The shallow ports, the simple sheltered inlets,
had seen their centuries of usefulness out.
Their reaches could be left to elvers and herons,
and kids with jam-jars.

In fact that didn't happen. Like a well
with buckets, one trade emptied, another filled.
The piles of slates and mounds of china clay,
the waiting carts,

these went, and with them went the wind-dried men
whose memories held the Horn, the snow, the icebergs,
the salt-caked clothes, the rats and cockroaches,
and as they ebbed

the new tide swirled in Dormobiles and trailers
to the trim week-end hulls. Bank managers
discussed tide-tables with psychiatrists.
Absurd? Of course,

but Charles, we recognize the hunger there,
the need for that ancient wrestle with the sea.
Man seeks a humanly intelligible danger:
something to test

his fibre against. His economic life
is trapped in a dead cocoon of filing-cards,
computers, plastics. Nothing in his survival
dictates that he,

his siblings or descendants, should ever go
anywhere near the sea; the populace, indeed,
who take their trips abroad from inland airports,
have, for the most part,

never been on a ship. But memory lives
more strongly in bone-marrow than in the cells
of the wakeful brain. In all the coastal peoples
of Western Europe

a man or a woman here and there goes back
to the tides, the cliffs, the swell, where life depends
on staying awake enough to read a compass.
Often, in fog,

the looming tankers run them down: in storm,
waves rip out their aluminium masts. Where once
men stood and looked at the mocking waves and thought,
*Face them, or starve*,

now starving has nothing to do with sailing, they come
to challenge the sea again, to dip and scurry,
and even dare the Atlantic in craft as frail
as bicycles,

and though they look funny, Charles, with their yellow
gum-boots and little vanities, you and I find them
worth saluting as, dodging assorted monsters,
they ride the sea-lanes.

# Ode to a Nightingale

It's your sense of theatre, we realise, inconspicuous
drab brown communicator, that does it, your choice of
space and occasion to set off your performance:
that resplendent fame

didn't come to you in straight competition, for even
a cloth-eared amateur like me can discern that
in terms of pure aesthetics the thrush and the blackbird
in their ordinary urban

settings, back garden and chimney-pot, performing
at routine times when the sun is climbing or sinking,
make music that note for note need fear no comparison
with your artfullest descant;

what makes you a star is your *penchant* for shade and seclusion,
not mere dusk but the last hour of slow-motion nightfall
in June when the daylight has all but abolished the darkness,
yet part of that all-but

is the thrilling aria you launch unannounced from somewhere
one's eyes can seldom penetrate. Your love of the covert
adds that dimension of mystery all art needs; it's as well
not to parade your

act in the sunlight, for, besides the more bustling
competition, there is your totally unremarkable
appearance, the bird-world's equivalent of
our brief-cased commuters.

Our species could learn from you, except that we can't
learn from anything, being vain and unteachable.
We prod our artists into the spotlight, bring up
cameras and mikes

to record their banalities, place on embarrassing record
their threadbare opinions; like you, they're predictably
humdrum except when performing, but unlike you
they simply don't see it.

No, little brown bird, go on wisely ignoring
our foolish example; as you have been, continue:
from your shadowy perch, make the night grow reckless with music.
By your art we shall know you.

# Prospero's Staff in the Earth

> '. . . I'll break my staff,
> Bury it certain fathoms in the earth,
> And deeper than did ever plummet sound
> I'll drown my book.'

The drowned book, yes;
I see it sifting down:
the paper bunching like seaweed
then riffling, opening,
showing its pages in the subacqueous light,
showing its symbols to the staring cod
and the expressionless lobster:
the stitched spine holding,
the ink not fading because it was magic ink,
the round o's of the figures like eyes
staring up at the feet of sea-birds,
floating and swaying between sea and sky:
and in the end shredding out,
dwindling to wisps of pulp,
the stored thoughts veining into ocean-streams,
brooks of knowledge in the thick salt gloom,
defined channels of wisdom, but not permanent,
dispersed, dispersed, and in the end forgotten:
all this I can see.

But the staff in the earth!
'certain fathoms' suggests meditation,
suggests calculation, an arrived-at point
below the pathways of mole and beetle,
below the drinking-threads of casual shrubs,
its grave neighbours the roots of the strong trees,
just above the level of the hardest rocks:
just above our planet's carapace.

Were the grains astonished?
In the silence that came down after the magician,
up there in the evening light, had walked away,
having murmured the last incantations,
the valedictions:
when tall Prospero, without staff or book,
turned his face naked to the sunset's fire,
and the grains that held the newcomer
were left to their long vigil.
These grains also had their dignity, their stored
and memoried selves were of many noble kinds;
there was the self of milled rock, and of humus,
end of the seasonal mould of leaves:
end of the long-dispersed flesh of animals
and birds: and their bones, which were not dispersed,
but lay quietly in their original diagrams,
the structure of their first agile inheritors:
almost as quietly as the stones, with their calm
vocabulary of stillness.
                    Did the stranger
startle or challenge the bones and grains?

Everything about it was strange.
What was the bark? What was the grained wood?
What tree nourished it, and when
let it fall?

Surely that was an unknown tree.
What soil held its roots? Not the soil
of this place, or any place
visited by sailors.

Was it single, the only tree of its kind.
or were there six in a ring
in some secret place of the world?
What jewelled birds perched there,
or were they dark, hooded birds?

63

Was there transformation?
Did the staff change slowly into something else?
And as it changed, did it impart its knowledge
a throb at a time to the hard roots about it,
till one by one its atoms fell away:
till in the end there was only the memory
that a core of secrets once lay in the earth
in a spot that was marked with no memorial,
only a patch of soil like any other?
And, up in the light and air, a grove of trees
alive with birds, the ordinary common birds?

Perhaps it happened that way. Perhaps not.
And perhaps that was not the most important thing.

The most important thing was the forgiveness.

The staff was buried because the quarrel was.

The magic died with no one left to hate.

It was the cheated man who studied runes:
on the atoll of his rejection he brooded over spells
that pulled into the drag of vengeance-tides
the usurer's hull, his masts, his decks, his people.

The quiet grass grows over battlefields:
gentle slopes we walk on, cow-pastures
soaked up hot blood once, rang with hideous yells
of agony or equally hideous joy.

The peaceful grass grows on. This is the miracle.
Where Cain struck Abel down, the daisy's eye
opens each dawn in accustomed innocence.
So on the island of Prospero's rough magic
the polished staff put knowledge in the earth,
the highest knowledge and yet the commonest, fragrant

as breath of cows, majestic as the clouds.

While off the rocky point, the book sways down
to the sea-bed, and the magician's house
feels once again the pulse of life, the warmth,
the healing flesh, the young man and the girl.

# I'm Talking About Wildlife, What Are You Talking About?

Conservationists, sentimental conservationists,
always going on about wildlife:
they prefer animals to people.

Well, who doesn't?
I mean actually who doesn't
prefer animals to people?

Take that nattily-suited
businessman over there:
the one who's just ordered fillet steak.

He will pay more for a thick juicy steak
than he would dream of giving away
to a pallid child in the street,

and the steak is part of an animal:
only a small part, perhaps,
but the part he's interested in.

Yes, fine, the animal's dead.
Animals have to be dead
before they can interest him.

Killed, cooked, carved up
and lying on a plate:
how his eyes light up then!

Or take Miss World.
You know, that expensive line-up
of thighs, breasts and bottoms, teeth and hair.

The girls with those big anxious smiles
show themselves off so prettily,
move prettily, go through their pretty tricks.

We can only see them as animals,
healthy, groomed, nurtured animals;
we don't get to *talk* to them.

And the one who wins is the best animal.
Well, isn't she?
If she isn't an animal, what is she then?

So the men who set it all up,
who advertise, who promote, who spend fortunes,
also prefer animals to people.

Conservationists? They're playing at it.
In the business of preferring animals
to people, they're just beginners.

They think people would respect themselves more
if they left animals in peace. What a laugh!
Who leaves girls or beefsteaks in peace?

# As a Child, I Saw the R101

1

I was playing in our front garden.
'Playing' for me at that time
usually meant being close to the ground,
something that involved crouching
attentive to pebbles, grains of sand,
to the grass-blades trembling like a forest,
a thin green jungle loaded with surprises,
complete with predators, with escapers and hiders.
It meant being intimate with surfaces,
distinguishing colours and textures. Ours was
a sandstone area, the earth was dark red.
In wet weather the soil thickened to clay.
You could have kneaded it, baked shallow pots.
Playing meant kinship with chips of wood, bark-peel,
cement paths cool and smooth after being swept:
dandelions invading through gaps in the fence,
gold-shining uninvited guests.
                              It was mid-morning,
so the fact that I was playing in the garden
dates it before 1930, that tight-lipped year
when I put on school clothes and said goodbye to
solitary connoisseurship of ground textures:
had to sit up to a desk and forget about
earth-grains, pebbles, the dark red soil,
had to run about in a playground and forget
the thin green jungle stalking with big game.

It must have been before that, this morning,
in the days when I was small and close to the ground,
when I went to the earth for companionship
and my adventures were among the grass-blades.

The R101 made no noise. And in
our quiet cul-de-sac there were no knot of uplookers
turning to call in at open doors and windows
'Father! Doris! Come and see the airship!'

I was alone in the quiet morning,
busy with leaves and pebbles, spiders, grains:
and then I happened to look up and see it.


2

It seemed so low it hardly cleared the houses:
so leisurely, so open to inspection
drawn gently on by tamed and harnessed forces
it moved so calmly in its planned direction.

It floated like a ship. How could that be?
I felt a sudden need to hug the ground.
So huge, and sailing there so weightlessly,
it turned the air to water. I was drowned.

The space above the house, above the trees
had always been free space: flight-path for birds
a sieve for raindrops, playground of the breeze,
cloud-architect. Now, out of reach of words,

an unknown panic stirred in me, and woke:
my veins were gripped by a new chill of dread:
something prophetic touched my strings and spoke
as Laputa came sailing overhead.

And since that morning I have come to see
that I inhabit the troubled dream of Swift:
the calm, the mad, the doomed effrontery
of minds that trust the mindless wind, and drift.


3

What am I saying? That man ought never to venture?
The brain-washed chatter of those who have swallowed the sinker
of Progress is wearisome; still, the stubborn refusal to budge
is wearisome also:

69

it smacks of sulking, that mulish determination
not to respond to discovery, or to concede that
life-styles can ever improve. On the face of it, no,
I would never join forces

with those so bewitched by the bloodless stone-like beauty
of immobility that they blame their parents
for reaching out further than grandparents did, who
think of technology

as I think of cancer. I like the White Knight
in Alice: now he, for one, would have found
a lovely mad poetry in taking his seat in a huge
silver cigar-tube

and riding in it to view the cloudscape. Yes,
wild notions, if they succeed, become prosy and solid,
like blocks of flats on the fringes of cities. But this
one didn't. About the time

when I started going to school and learning that life
meant coping with fools and bullies and bending one's spirit
to crush through the rigid bars of rule and convention,
so also mankind

sat down in a hard-bench classroom where under the tyrant
Fire, they learnt to drop the rose-coloured dream
of a five-star hotel held aloft by a huge container
of inflammable gas.

The Edwardian age of flight with its quaint Heath-Robinson
contraptions, its dreams of luxury liners (armchair
service and ping-pong rooms) in the azure, was fried
in those terrible bonfires:

flight now means five-mile runways, and screaming wide-bodied
jets. And even before I had lived another
ten years, Guernica, and the Luftwaffe, and Mitchell
designing the Spitfire.

It was an old dream that died the death
annihilated on an agony's anvil.
Of so piteous a peak of human pain
we must not speak: a sad silence
is the only mercy in that mass mutilation.
But how strong-standing, what a stayer
was that darling-dream of a daintier life –
how vivid that vision of a stately vessel
floating freely, no fear of falling
nor any noise, nor noxious haste
to dock on time at some drear destination:
to stroll her carpeted corridors, and calmly
look through her lofty windows at the lake
of blue with its white billows, its soft balloons,
to partake of this was life at her pride's peak!
once down, dismasted, they would be doomed
to trudge on two feet like troglodytes:
the biped beasts they knew themselves to be,
and disdained the knowledge. Down, down,
swift hound of satire: compassion, speak,
for the dream these savoured was simple and shining,
grounded as deep as man's grasping at godhead:
all those plumed pinions of angels planing
down from the domes of Deity's H.Q.
with terse messages for muddled mankind,
or, in the clear Greek air, the green grounding
of the oligarchs of Olympus about their off-hand
trade with us human trash. Transient, in truth,
their earthward fancies and furies, the force
of their satyr's lust for lissom limbs
or vicious vendetta against some violator
who had pushed at the palings of their privilege –

but constant their compulsion to compromise,
by incessant intervention, our inwardness.
Poor as our pleasure was, they wanted a piece of it.
That, at least, is how the ever-living
seemed to our dreams and our devout designs.
We saw them as air-borne: their effortless ascent
to the tranquil sky was the true sign
that they were the gods and we the grumbling groundlings
clogged to the dour clods of sour clay.
But I didn't mind: I never missed those manoeuvres
in the free-dimensional field of fine floating:
the pebbles I coaxed and counted, crouched in the garden,
were my world of truth: I trusted no trimaran,
galleon, grain-clipper or grim grey frigate
to liberate my life into a loose-knit lightness.
To clamber up clown-high among clustering leaves,
braced against bark, gave enough of the bright
sky for me to taste, to touch and treasure:
a spider-web on a still morning, dew-silvered,
or the luminous white of a pebble, light-laced
with veins of red, was verity's voice.


So farewell, R101, flimsy enfolder
of a race's reveries, follow your route
towards (and I pity it) the preordained pyre,
that murder-flash mast-flame of flesh;
and Earth, home and haven, receive my homage
for ever, even as on that overlooked morning
when, craning up at the incomprehensible cruiser,
I found my refuge in your rough-coated roots.

# Enjoyable Poem

It doesn't seem likely, now,
that I shall live to be eighty: as I once
announced my intention of doing.

I announced it to a newspaper
that interviewed me when I was forty.
'I'm half-way,' I said.

Twenty-one years later,
it seems pretty obvious
I can forget about that one.

Bothered by this and that,
taking tablets for that and this,
ageing, slow, plagued in the flesh.

But then, why should I, more than another,
rear a majestic arch of years
on this ailing planet?

A lot of useless bores
hang on for supererogatory decades,
to the faint annoyance of those about them.

My most admired friend,
Philip of the truthful Eeyore-vision,
lived just sixty-three years.

Burly Ernest Hemingway,
whose play-acting and posing I despised,
but not his economical pen,

went out at sixty-two.
In his case, the mind jumped first,
pulling the body with it,

but the effect was the same.
The effect always is the same –
last week they were here, this week they're not.

Just so, in no very long time,
I shall go, like them, here this week,
next week, an absence.

Will anyone notice?
Well, *I* shan't know
whether they notice or not,

which is the only justification
for speculating now, as I sit
in the sun, before lunch, with a drink.

I suppose, looking at it objectively,
I have been noticed, at least now and then:
in some quarters, at least.

I have to assume that during my life-span
my influence made itself felt
to some few among the Established,

since they made me a Commander
of the British Empire (long after
there was any B.E. to command,

except of course the Malvinas/Falklands,
though I did little to help with that:
not feeling the South Atlantic to be home ground).

I never wanted to command empires,
but I would have liked to have some influence
on the great structure of thought and language

we call a civilization:
and when I am gone there will be one fewer
who cares a rat's tooth about civilization.

It is something you package for television,
or into coffee-table books,
but not something you let into your bloodstream:

it might do you harm there, like AIDS,
by making you vulnerable.
I was vulnerable.

Yes, perhaps that's what I would want
as an epitaph,
not to be cut in stone,

or any of that nonsense,
but just carried around in people's heads:
*he was vulnerable.*

He could be pierced so easily,
pierced, wounded, infected,
infected with death, infected with joy and life.

Always so easily pierced!
so unforewarned, so unguarded,
indeed, making almost

a *métier* of being exposed:
no professional mask, no grease-paint,
no hand-carved niche,

no job, no title, no pension;
reasonably well known, but no fame:
industrious enough to be solvent, mostly,

but never rich: no bunker
and no defences:
like, vulnerable!

And if he achieved now and then
something strong, it was by being open
to everything life threw towards him.

But that's enough boasting.
Having been vulnerable doesn't make me holy:
I just couldn't help it.

I would have been glad enough to be *rusé*,
to watch for my chances, to grab sinecures,
to marry money,

to elbow the competition into the gutter
and then say 'Really, we must do something
about that awful gutter

full of all those failed people.
We must be good, *concerned*, caring.'

Eff your concern, I always felt
like saying to them,
and sometimes did:

but that's me boasting again.
I called this 'Enjoyable Poem:'
the title came first,

because I intended to make it
the kind of poem that is fun to write,
and, possibly, mild fun to read,

though for once I was less intent on that.
Forty years I have worked for my readers,
trying to have the good manners

not to baffle them, or tie them
in gratuitous knots, to say clearly
whatever *could* be said clearly, to do

the heavy work and not leave it to them:
well, reading this poem (if anyone
has got this far) won't have been

heavy work; it should flow like a letter
to an old friend one feels easy with,
and after all,

that's what England is to me:
an old friend, faults and all,
whatever happens.

# The Shipwreck
## For a Painting by J. M. W. Turner

This canvas yells the fury of the sea.
Across a quiet room, where people murmur
their poised appreciations, it shrieks out
the madness of the wind.
                              How can that be?
Woven of voiceless threads, its pigments laid
with 'no more sound than the mice make', it hurls
the tempest at my eardrums, and my eyes
smart in the lashing spray. But not before
the colours of tragedy have enkindled them:
it must be so, because the colours hold
the secret. They are noise, and tilt, and steepness.
The colours are trough, and crash, the cry of gulls
lifted and blown away like part of the spume.
The colours are the bawling of the wind.
That yellow sail, its mast snapped sideways, catches
into itself and holds that gleam of light
amid the livid waters, the evening gleam
through torn black cloud as the sullen day departs.
One last message of life. Over and out.
The people in the small escaping boat
(too frail for the uncaring slide and smash
of those tall water-cliffs, promising only
ten minutes more of life, of clinging on
before the toppling plunge) see in that yellow
the last of life that they will ever see.
A goodbye signal, perhaps a welcoming
to those new neighbours, whoever they will be,
who wait for them on the other side of darkness,
below the clap of the waves and lace of foam
down there in the dark, and then below the dark,
in the calm of the still depths (the most tremendous
storm makes no disturbance below nine fathoms).
Will their new world be down on the ocean-floor,

among the caves? Or, following the blown gulls,
through some still gleaming crevice of the sky?
Or will they start again on the green earth,
as newts this time, or leaning-tower giraffes,
or crocodiles who lie still as old tyres
in estuary mud? Or human children
with different facial bones and frizzy hair?
Or will they be the atoms of the water
next time, and hammer some trim ketch to planks
and floating spars? Will they be starfish, lying
five-pointed on the beach these voyagers
would give, in this death-minute, everything
they ever owned to be treading, calmly, now?
Who knows? What we can ask, I think, is
whether death will seem beautiful to them when it comes,
and to us, for that matter, after the pain
is over, I mean. Many great artists have
extolled the beauty of death, have loved and called to it,
and Turner here seems to be saying *Now*
*I will show you how terror and agony*
*and the utterly final arrival of death can distil*
*an essence of beauty-in-terror, an enrichment*
*in the moment of final relinquishment of all*:
as if it took that knowledge, that edge of torment,
to peel away the cataract from our vision,
to reveal the beauty of those mad waters
and that last gleam of light from a hostile day.
Meanwhile, one thing I know: the silent canvas
has stored the howl and thunder of that hour,
the yell of death in the ears of the sacrificed:
the last groan of the timbers, the frantic slap
of the saturated sail. Canvas to canvas. Sound
to silence, through the artist's compassionate mind,
and back to sound again, as I stand here.

Oh, it has 'painterly values' too, and can be discussed
in purely abstract terms: but not now, not now.
Some other time, not in the presence of
the human creatures, air-breathers, gulping their last,
and the sea's roaring that never will be quenched,
and beyond, the starfish at his supine vigil
on the final beach whose shingle we shall be.